THE
BLUFFER'S GUIDE®
TO
THE CLASSICS

ROSS LECKIE

O

Oval Books

Published by Oval Books
335 Kennington Road
London SE11 4QE
United Kingdom

Telephone: +44 (0)20 7582 7123
Fax: +44 (0)20 7582 1022
E-mail: info@ovalbooks.com

First published by Ravette Publishing, 1989
Reprinted, 1992, 1993

New edition published by Oval Books, 1999
Reprinted 1999, 2000

Series Editor – Anne Tauté

Cover designer – Jim Wire, Quantum
Printer – Cox & Wyman Ltd
Producer – Oval Projects Ltd

The Bluffer's Guides® series is based
on an original idea by Peter Wolfe.

The Bluffer's Guide®, The Bluffer's Guides®,
Bluffer's®, and Bluff Your Way®
are Registered Trademarks.

Dedication: For A C-T

'Is it not great to be a King, Techellas,
Is it not passing great to be a King,
And ride in triumph through Persepolis?'

ISBN: 1-902825-48-9

CONTENTS

Dramatis Personae

INTRODUCTION

In these days of scholars of Peace Studies and BAs (Hons) in Countryside Recreation Participation, there has never been a better or easier time to become a distinguished bluffer in the Classics. As Greece comes to mean holidays and Italy pasta, as fewer and fewer people know or care who Homer was or what Brutus did, the opportunities for dazzling bluff in the Classics have become limited only by your imagination.

In many bluffs, you run the risk of coming across someone who might spot you. With the Classics, you may assume a reckless confidence, subject only to avoiding dinners in Oxbridge colleges. That shouldn't be too difficult. Even then you have much on your side – Oxbridge dons can never agree about anything, and if you stick to a really safe bluff, like Aristotle, you can't go wrong: no-one knows what he meant anyway, either in Greek or English. Claim that Plato was a Marxist or Virgil a freemason. Either would win you valuable time. And be sure to digress. The Greeks did it. The Romans did it. This book does it, even deliberately (sometimes). Every good Classical bluffer does it, for digression is the acme of his trade: it's the way to make a little knowledge go a long, long way.

Outside the academic world, bluffed or otherwise, the Classics will win you widespread respect. To be something of a Classicist is to align yourself with a time when Britain was Great and Men had Bottle. You immediately identify yourself with such respected fallacies as Democracy, Justice, Wisdom and Freedom. You grow in stature and become, somehow, that most desirable and mysterious of creatures, an Intellectual, for you have an Enquiring Mind and know your Alphas from your Omegas. You might even be able to spell.

The most hardened Philistine, happily ignorant of Schoenberg or the Impressionists, can still be made to feel slightly guilty if he knows nothing of the Classics. Tell him about the pre-Socratics' ontological elenchus. He'll love you for it.

Dazzle dull drinks parties by correcting, peremptorily, anyone rash enough to define 'Classicism' or, worse still, 'Neoclassicism'. For you will know that the former is but an omelette made of Greek eggs and the latter but an omelette made of reconstituted Greek eggs; that the former is concerned with something the Greeks discovered, the nude, but that the latter is much more complex, concerned as it is with the half-clothed nude.

Both, you will assert, are what cultures die of, for they reject innovation and epitomise the recidivism with which our prisons are full. If you are in absolutely top form, you might mention the origins of Classicism in the *'Enkekrimenoi'*, those authors whose works were 'Admitted' to the great 2nd century BC library at Alexandria, promptly burnt down by Julius Caesar because he was in a huff with Cleopatra.

So tell your bank manager that it's really very desirable to live like Croesus. He might consider 'character lending'. Impress those endless political conversations by describing contemporary democracy as 'Peisistratean'. It sounds good, is true, will offend few and impress many.

Don't make your bluff, then, the pistes of Switzerland or the history of the Baltic States. For less work and more effect, make it the Classics.

WHEN?

You should consider it your good fortune that, if you don't know what period of history is meant by 'the Classics', no-one else does either. Indeed, you could do worse than specialise in this vexed question. It could last you for years.

If you were able to find one eloquent enough, a Professor of Classics (helpfully known at Oxford as 'Literae Humaniores') might reply: "The Classical Period begins somewhere in the 8th century BC and ends somewhere in the 2nd century AD." You get the general idea. Ask with which historical event the Classics begin or end, and you will receive hours of impressively incomprehensible bluff.

It is always a good idea to introduce the thoughts of a German Classical scholar on this (or any other) subject. You can be sure that no-one will contradict you, because they won't have read him either. Use 'von Wilamowitz-Moellendorf' extensively. It trips off the tongue, sounds good and he did exist. No-one, though, understands his German, let alone his thoughts on the Classics.

You might also want to try the 'termini' approach. 'Termini' is the plural of the Latin word for boundary. Thus you get 'terminus ante quem' and 'terminus post quem', the boundary before and after which something was. **Homer** is always a safe bet for the post quem. That is to say, you might define the Classics as beginning with and after Homer.

Alternatively, and if you're very good, you might define it as beginning 'haud ante Homerum', that is to say 'not before Homer'. If you're feeling especially mischievous, bring **Hesiod**, as in 'the Hesiodic terminus', into play. We do, at least, know that he existed, which is more than can be said of Homer. The trouble is, we don't really know when.

If the beginning of 'the Classics' is bad, the ending is even worse. Stick your neck out. Define the end of the Classical Age as when the Emperor Hadrian (AD 117-38) first developed a predilection for donkeys and for walls. That will lead you, at once, to the sort of subjects on which your imagination and people's interest will flourish.

If all this begins to fatigue you or your audience, you have two absolutely safe bets.

I. The first is to claim that 'the Classis' is a myth. The Classical period of Greece, you might say, is merely the 'pentekonta etea' of Athens, the '50 years' between the Persian (490 BC) and the Peloponnesian (431 BC) Wars. The missing years will allow you to expound upon the inexactitudes of chronology and medieval monks, and you can always blame **Thucydides**. Write off Sparta, Corinth, Thebes and other minor, tiresome places. These years, you can claim, gave us the Parthenon, Aeschylus and homosexuality, and all the rest is bosh. This has the merits of being definitive, pellucid – and completely wrong.

As for the Romans, say that their Classical period is simply that of **Augustus**, from his victory over Antony and Cleopatra at Actium in 31 BC to his death and deification in AD 14. Again, it's roughly 50 years, sounds good, is tidy and, at least, takes in **Virgil**.

Hint at your knowledge of Augustus' 'Pax Romana' (the Roman peace). Ignore Tacitus' view of this: 'Solitudinem faciunt, pacem appellant' (They made a desert and they called it a peace). This is called an antithesis and it's true, but it didn't worry Dryden or Pope and doesn't worry members of the EU so it can't be important.

Refer copiously to Augustus' many laws, clear proof that the Augustan was, indeed, the Classical and Golden Age. For instance:

a) There was so much promiscuity that Augustus' *Lex Iulia de Adulteriis* (18 BC) made adultery a public crime.
b) There was so little legitimate procreation that the *Lex Iulia de Maritandis Ordinibus* (17 BC) made marriage all but compulsory.
c) There was so much discipline and asceticism that the old man had to pass his *Lex Sumptuaria*, banning 'extravagant luxury'.

All good stuff.

If all else fails, bring in a German: refer with bated breath to H.B. Meyer's seminal and monumental *Die Aussenpolitik des Augustus und die Augusteische Dichtung*, your source for whatever you want. Yet you must take care: someone might have heard of Republican Rome or have been conned by Cicero into believing that it, and not the Augustan Age, was Rome's Classical period.

If this happens, you will deploy a 'reductio ad absurdum'. Agree that there is some evidence to suggest that the Romans of the Republic were, indeed, solid chaps. Relate exempli gratia, how, when the all-conquering Hannibal camped his army (elephants, actually) at the very walls of Rome in 211 BC for a quick smoke before the city's certain sack, these Republican Romans auctioned the ground on which the army (elephants, actually) was encamped. It fetched its normal price.

But then begin your 'reduction to the absurd', and with care and guile refer to the glories of Republican Rome in literature (there was none), in art (there was none), in architecture (there was none). Republican Rome was full of wise, tolerant men – like Cato the Censor. Democracy flourished, in the form of the Comitia Centuriata whose *Lex Hortensia* (287 BC) granted adult male suffrage. The Comitia then did absolutely nothing until 200 years later, when it appointed Sulla dictator (82 BC).

Observe that Scipio's great victory over Antiochus the Great and his Seleucid Empire in 189 BC may, indeed, have given Rome world domination, but it hardly gave the world 'the Classics'. The Romans were much too busy with other things, like slavery. They enslaved 80,000 Sardinians in 176 BC and 150,000 Epirotes in 167 BC so were much too busy building slave markets to be Classicists. So much for Republican Rome.

But you shouldn't worry too much whether 'the Classics' in Rome was the Republican or the Augustan period, since it wasn't either. Your original point (that 'the Classics' is a myth) stands. This is known as sophistry and it works.

II. Your second bet is to claim that "the Classics have never died but live on, e.g. in the Marsh Arabs' fight for freedom in Iraq or in the tolerance of Gadaffi. They were, in the beginning, in the Garden of Eden, they were when Britannia ruled the waves and peace will come, etc." This will allow you to seem something of a philosopher, a Classical and compelling bluff.

You won't, of course, have answered the question 'When?' but you will console yourself by murmuring the immortal words of **Zenas of Sardis**: "The clash of the over-credulous and the over-sceptical must continue for the benefit of the resulting golden mean."

WHERE?

In answer to the question 'Where?' your best gambit, as always, is a bold one. Deny categorically that the Classical world was Greece or Italy and do so, for once, in the knowledge that you're right. Claim, without being too unreasonable, that the Classical world stretched from the Antonine Wall in Scotland to the Great Wall of China (almost), though not at the same time.

Greece

Assure your rapt listeners that 'Greece' never existed. It was merely a motley collection of independent, bickering city-states (poleis to you, and that's plural) – Athens, Sparta, Thebes, Argos, Corinth and so on (inter alias to you) – which spent most of their time knocking hell out of each other. The only time they ever got together was for the four-yearly (quadrennial to you) Olympic Games (founded in 776 BC and extended to five days, not weeks and weeks, in 472 BC) when they competed furiously, either running about in full armour, or naked, in order to win chaplets of olive leaves. There were no team events and each state's (polis to you, and that's singular) competitors certainly didn't strut about in spivlon blazers. But then they hadn't seen *Chariots of Fire*.

These city states of 'Greece' had different sexual practices, gods and laws. Their languages and dialects were so different that our word 'solecism' (bad grammar) is from the people of Soli, an Athenian colony whose language was incomprehensible to everyone, especially to the Athenians.

What the poleis had in common were eastern enemies who were called satraps and wandered about with cleavers. Even then, they couldn't get together – when Darius, Super Satrap of Persia (521-486 BC) landed his great army at Marathon in 490 BC, determined to annihilate the 'Greeks', only the abject Plataeans responded to Athens' embarrassed request for a little assistance.

Athens sent a runner, one Pheidippides, to Sparta to ask for help, but the Spartans were engaged in one of their interminable religious festivals and said they might turn up later. They did, but the battle was over. Some good came of it, though: by running the 120 miles to Athens in two days, Pheidippides gave masochists and insane Finns the 'marathon' and had a vision of the God Pan in transit.

If your audience is especially erudite, someone might dare to challenge your thesis by referring to the leagues and confederations that weren't Greece but were a shambles – the Peloponnesian League (500 BC), the Delian League (478 BC) and the Amphictyonic League, whenever anyone could spell it. This shameless braggart might argue that, in these leagues, 'Greece' did exist. Do not waver. The leagues were used by their founders as some politicians now use parliaments. They were as effective as ceasefires in Serbia and lasted about as long as politicians' promises.

So strong was the fraternity of the Peloponnesian League that, by statute, if there was no League war in progress, members were free to make war on each other. And when a meeting of the Delian League was convened to discuss the rebuilding of Greece's temples (destroyed during the Persian war) nobody turned up. Just like the UN, really.

Now you are on the home stretch, at least as far as 'Greece' is concerned. If you need them, though, you have two more, insuperable arguments: Colonies and Sparta.

Colonies

The 'archaic period' (776-500 BC) saw each polis replicate itself like a mutant cell, none more so than the maritime poleis which had less land than Liechtenstein: Corinth, Megara, Chalcis. Refer, naturally, to **Herodotus**: 'Greece and poverty were foster-sisters', which at least goes to prove that some things don't change.

As they bred, legitimately or otherwise, the poleis needed more land. Sparta simply whipped it from its neighbours and Athens hoped the problem would go away. The gentler poleis were more decisive. They just threw vast groups of their beloved citizens out. These colonies spread to France, Spain, Cyrene, Egypt and Asia Minor, a Southern Italian group becoming known as 'Magna Graecia' (Big Greece). There must be a moral somewhere.

But you still haven't found Greece – Magna, Parva or, indeed, at all. This is because, even by 600 BC, it would be as accurate to describe 'Greece' as Greece as to call the Hapsburg Empire Vienna. Alexander the Great made the matter even more difficult by extending the boundaries of 'Greece' to India. The Hellenistic Kingdoms consolidated his conquests until they, too, were gobbled up by Roman fascism, sorry, Classicism, although, as **Horace** says, 'Graecia capta ferum victorem cepit et artes intulit agresti Latio' ('Captive Greece took her fierce conqueror captive and introduced the arts to rustic Latium'). And for once he was right.

Whether or not it's relevant, you should make much of this point of Horace's. Remember that, as a Classical bluffer, you will always have the benefit of any doubt; people will invariably assume that your point is complex, rather than irrelevant, unless you are really very stupid about it. If reluctantly forced to agree that the Classical world was somewhere, say: "It was in Greece, wherever that was... Perhaps Greece was in her colonies; perhaps, as Horace observes, it was in Rome, where everything was Greek except for law, concrete and straight roads." For good bluffers in the Classics must master the Classical technique of never making a statement when asking a question will do.

As a parting shot, you should maintain that even when Rome went down before the barbarians in the 5th century AD, the 'Greek' world survived for many more centuries as the Eastern Roman (Byzantine) Empire. This must be true. That great luminary Baron von Ow zu Essen von Wachendorf says so, somewhere.

Sparta

At last you turn to Sparta. If ever there were proof that the poleis of 'Greece' were too weird ('iconoclastic' to you) to constitute anything, let alone Greece, that proof is Sparta, a state which managed to display not one of the characteristics that we think of as (archetypally) 'Greek' and none of those that we think of as 'Classical'. No thinkers, no temples, no theatre, no democracy, no literature, not even the odd vase and certainly no alcohol.

You should get away with that one, unless (and it's unlikely) someone has heard of Sparta's only two scribblers, Tyrtaeus and Alcman. One wrote turgid stuff along the lines of 'Get out there and get 'em, boys'. The other wrote verse to prepare Spartan women for marriage, 'Obey and breed'. Dismiss them both.

Return to your theme. Sparta makes Hitler's Reich look like a registered charity. Its society was formed of three, simple classes: the ruling Spartan men, Spartiates (some 4,000), serfs (Helots) and semi-serfs (Perioekoi). India has absolutely nothing to worry about. Sparta renounced both trade and foreign contacts. It devoted itself to the breeding and training of soldiers by way of a system which killed most female babies at birth and left all males outside, unwrapped, for a night or two. Those who survived might be worth training. Whilst other Greek states were posturing with democracy, Sparta enhanced monarchy. It prohibited emigration or immigration.

A Sybarite, entertained at the public mess at Sparta, remarked: 'Now I understand why the Spartans do not fear death.' Another visitor, faced with a bowl of Spartan broth, said: 'You need a swim in the Eurotas before you can eat this.' After a long siege, the Plataeans surrendered to the Spartans on the terms that 'they should submit to the Spartans as their judges, who would punish the guilty, but none contrary to justice.' The Spartan idea of justice (something the 'Greeks' were supposed to be keen on) was to ask each Plataean whether, during the war, he had done anything to help Sparta. A Plataean spokesman reminded the Spartans that it would be surprising if any of them had helped Sparta, since they were on the other side. The Spartans promptly killed all the men, sent the women into slavery and razed the city to the ground. Those were the days.

Sparta, you will argue, was in 'Greece', but was not 'Greek' and, therefore, Greece was not. This is rubbish, but appears subliminally logical and, therefore, plausible. Try it, anyway.

Italy and Rome

Your argument for Italy, mercifully, is much simpler. You could, of course, attempt to maintain that the 'where?' of the Roman Classical world was from sea to shining sea, behind every bush and under every hypocaust; you could refer to the 'immensa Romanae pacis maiestas' – the boundless majesty of the Roman peace. But you won't, for you know, if others don't, that all the Romans did was build the odd road, send in a few legions, beat up the odd peasant and banish some poor fellow from Rome to run the place. You would, yourself, tire of life in Andalucia and weary of the culture of Sergovium.

Plump, unerringly, for Rome. No-one who was anyone ever wanted to be anywhere else. An appointment outside Rome was as popular as the Welsh Office. Anything that the Romans did that was 'Classical' was pinched from the Greeks anyway (apart from law, concrete and straight roads), but the centre of the counterfeit was always, always Rome. Italy was ante-pasta and the true Roman cared for Italy only in the spirit. For a Roman, life was 'Urbi et Orbi' (for the city and the world).

The great Empire, meanwhile, was simply:

a) a place in which to have dirty weekends (witness Nero's caves and their pornographic murals, whence the word 'grotesque')
b) the source of the money, slaves and bizarre sexual practices needed to keep Rome up.

Thus you will answer the question 'Where was the Classical world?' with exemplary, obfuscatory clarity: it wasn't in Greece, because Greece never was, and it wasn't in Italy or the Empire because Italy and the Empire were Rome, and it wasn't in Rome because Rome was Greece.

This should silence all but the most dogged, to whom you will say, changing tack completely: "The Classical world was wherever men asked 'Where am I?, Why am I here?, What am I doing?, What is the Good?' and wherever they then attempted to articulate the resulting confusion in some form of art, pornographic or otherwise."

You will assume a measured gravity here, for you know that our contemporary inability to ask such questions, let alone to get the right answers, should be worn as a badge of shame and is inimical to everything that was glorious in the Classical world. Sing, instead, of the joy of enquiry and the search for knowledge and the quest for the perfection of the whole, wherein lies the Classical world.

Quote **Sophocles**: 'Polla ta deina, kooden anthropoo deinoteron telei' (Wonders are many, but none is more wonderful than man).

WHO?

The dramatis personae of the Classical world divide neatly into three camps:

I. Those who definitely did not exist.
II. Those who almost existed.
III. Those who definitely did exist because they are now dead.

These categories are known to Classicists, bafflingly, as Gods, Demi-Gods and Men.

Though hardly exhaustive, quite unrepresentative and utterly subjective, this list should see any bluffer with an IQ over minus 10 through anything but the Annual General Meeting of the Classical Association. It includes several marked with a (B), on whom the bluffer should concentrate. They have passed every test as being of inordinate utility in illustrating any point whatsoever, since the only thing anyone knows about them is that they know nothing at all. Is that clear?

Gods

Your vital bluffers' word here is 'anthropomorphic': Greek and Roman Gods had the form of men, which means that they got drunk, were adulterous, libidinous and, generally, not Gods at all but men. The poet Xenophanes (floruit = was going strong, 545 BC), had the general idea when he observed that if oxen were religious, they would imagine their gods in the form of oxen. This may sound like common sense, but Xenophanes knew and you must remember one thing about common sense: it just isn't common.

Your second bluffers' word is 'dualism'. Observe that the 'theistic dualism' of the ancients was, like Caesar's Gaul, tripartite (at least) and neither the Greeks nor the Romans ever quite sorted this out. This is because:

i.   on the one hand their Gods really were Gods and yet, on the other, they could be men.
ii. on the one hand the Olympian Gods were the dominant lot, but, on the other, the older crowd like **Kronos** still had their part to play.
iii. the ancients (and especially the country bumpkins) continued to worship all kinds of obscure local Gods, nymphs, water-sprites, Lares, Penates and so on yet seemed to pay more than lip service to the First Division lot.

It's as if the Archbishop of Canterbury were also the Dalai Lama, an Ayatollah, the Maharishi Yogi, a warlock, believed in ley lines and remained an atheist. All very confusing, really, but, called 'dualism', excellent material for vintage bluff.

There are two more lines of fruitful and impressive argument open to you here:

I.   Wax lyrical about the capacity of the Classical world for 'polytheism' (belief in many Gods) and tolerance and contrast this, unfavourably, with modern monotheism (belief in one God) and intolerance. Religious persecution, evangelism, Moral Majorities,

Crusades, these were all but unknown in antiquity before Nero (whose antipathy towards the Christians was occasioned by anything but religion).

Allow yourself a brief discourse upon either the relative achievements of the two attitudes (one gives us the Parthenon, the other the Pompidou Centre), or the stranger of the many religious and orgiastic cults of the Classical world: Orphism, the Eleusinian Mysteries, Mithraism, Isis and Osiris and so on. Your point is, of course, that notwithstanding the variety and disparity of Classical religions and cults and the general hotchpotch thereof, these people still got out of bed in the morning and got on with being alive.

II. Your second option, should you decide to accept it, is arresting and controversial. In its favour, however, is the fact that there is some evidence to support it, and not just H.C. Bolkestein's (seminal and monumental) *Bijdrage tot de godsdienstige en zedelijke Terminologie van de Grieken* (1936).

This option entails the utter denial that the Classical world believed in God or Gods at all. (An extension to the argument is NOT to maintain that the Classical world believed in nothing, for as a Classical bluffer you will know that Nihilism is rot, since anyone who says he believes in nothing has said that he believes in something.)

Concentrate on the paradox: "At the throbbing heart of the Classical world lies the relentless search for abstract, enduring 'logos' (reason/order/meaning/purpose – Greek) or 'ratio' (a straight line – Roman). Yet we believe that these same searchers believed in and worshipped Gods who belched, fornicated, murdered and were generally pretty nasty or believed in and worshipped tree-sprites, earth-mothers and so on. How can this be?"

Ignore the fact that the Greeks and Romans at the

coal-face did make sense of this nonsense. Bring up the artillery. **Plato** thought that 'Gods' were made up by poets who should be exterminated and their Gods with them. Memorise and regularly quote a line from the poet **Ovid**:

'Expedit esse deos et, ut expedit, esse putemus.'
It is expedient that there should be Gods and, since it is expedient, let us think that there are.

Voltaire's cogged version was: 'If God did not exist, it would be necessary to invent him.'

Declare that the Classical world thought as much of Gods as Marx did. Most Roman Emperors just pronounced themselves Gods anyway and the really successful ancients, like the Epicureans and the Cynics and the Stoics, ignored Gods altogether. Meanwhile, as the Classical world aged, Fate (ate) and Chance (tuche) and Arrogance (hubris) and all sorts of abstract powers supplanted and mingled with the Gods and made the whole picture look even more surrealist.

Thus you can attempt to prove that the Classical world was an atheistic one and this, you will recall, was your second option. You may not have proved this at all. You may have proved the precise opposite. But you will at least have proved that the question of Classical attitudes to the Gods exemplifies the sort of complexity in which the ancients revelled and the moderns (except bluffers like you) get terribly, terribly lost.

Aphrodite
Greek Goddess of love, fertility, beauty and prostitution, Roman alias Venus. Born in the sea, her name, romantically, is from the Greek word 'aphros' (foam). To impress, you should concentrate upon her portfolio as Goddess of vegetation and chthonian deity; to interest, upon her patronage of prostitution and the

defloration of virgins before marriage.

You should stress her importance, nude, to Greek, Roman and later art. Praxiteles' 4th-century BC statue of her laying her robe on a hydria before taking a bath is the first convincing nude and playboys should be grateful to her. The Venus de Milo dominated the sexual fantasies of generations of schoolboys, many of whom are now cabinet ministers. Botticelli (c.1445-1510) and other artists made much of her, either wholly nude (Classicism) or almost (Neoclassicism).

Apollo

Gave his name to an absurdly expensive space programme which proved that Americans who can count backwards to zero are heroes. He was God of all sorts of things — music, archery, prophecy, medicine, the care of flocks, law and philosophy and must have been a busy man.

Yet he did not let the side down: Coronis, Cyrene and Cassandra were but three of his conquests whilst, meantime, he slew giants who were raping his mother, dragons and all that sort of thing. Usually naked and clutching a lyre or a bow, he is endlessly depicted.

Ares

God of war, son of Zeus and Hera, he sired an astonishing number of bastards which is surprising since he wasn't short of work. With Aphrodite he produced Deimos and Phobos, Rout and Fear, as well as Eros, Anteros and even Harmonia. Apart from being randy, he is generally dull and best dismissed by the serious bluffer. It is typical of the Romans that, as Mars, they made much of him.

Artemis

'Theriomorphic' (having the form of a beast) is really all you need to remember. It is as a beast that Artemis was worshipped. Daughter of Zeus, sister of Apollo and 'potnia theron', lady of wild things, her most remarkable attribute is her virginity. When Actaeon had the misfortune to come upon her bathing naked, she instantly turned him into a stag which was hunted and killed by hounds.

The Artemisian surprise at the Actaeon intrusion (good bluffer's phrases, these) was much considered by Tintoretto (1518-94) and Titian (obiit = pegged it, 1576). In his *Adonais*, Shelley made the whole tale bewilderingly complicated by seeing Artemis as Nature, Actaeon as his own mind and the hounds as his thoughts. You should recommend this as a homeopathic cure for insomnia.

Athena
The patron Goddess of Athens, she was insufferably wise, kind, diligent and interested in the finer things of life like spinning and weaving. She wasn't even born, but sprang, fully armed, from the head of Zeus. Hephaistos wanted to marry her and Zeus said he could try but she gave him little encouragement. She beat up Poseidon, too.

Female bluffers should be aware that if they find themselves called 'veritable Athena', they should not, whatever the circumstances or the lighting, construe this as a compliment.

Atlas (B)
Good bluffers should declare that the earlier Gods, the Titans, are much more interesting than the nouveaux like Zeus. Atlas was a Titan and a very good chap, patiently holding up the pillars of heaven in the days before *A Brief History of Time*. All his children are terribly nice – Kalypso, the Hesperides and the Pleiades. His name is from 'a' (intensive) and 'tlan' and means 'much enduring'. Absolutely right. We owe him one.

Bacchus

Otherwise known as Dionysus, God of wine and fertility, he had a bad start to life. Zeus begat him in a mere mortal, Semele. Hera, Zeus' wife, got very excited and had Semele consumed by one of Zeus' thunderbolts, but Zeus saved the foetus from its mother's ashes and stuck it in his thigh, from which Bacchus was born after a normal gestation.

Bluffers should know about Bacchus' drinking but concentrate on his orgies. He specialised in driving women mad and inspiring them to tear living people to pieces and eat them. This is called 'omophagy', but it has yet to catch on. One such orgy is well described in Euripides' play, *The Bacchae*.

Bacchus spent most of his working life surrounded by voluptuous women called Maenads, which must have been nice for someone. When sated with the Maenads he sought solace in Satyrs. Such were the size of their organs that no-one much cared they were half goat or that one of their number taught Achilles. Exactly what he was taught is one of your obsessions. Greek tragedy developed from Satyr plays and you will maintain that there's a moral there somewhere.

His orgies, known as Bacchanalia, continued in the Roman world. The Senate had to take special measures to repress them and their accompanying crime wave in 186 BC. This is an example of continuity in the Classics.

Hera

Juno to the Romans, she was a nasty, scheming piece, but then she had to live with Zeus. She also happens to have been Zeus' sister, which is a trifle tasteless. She spent most of her time wiping out Zeus' mistresses and bastards, so she was kept pretty busy. The only thing you should like about her is that she didn't like **Aeneas** (q.v.).

Kronos

King of the Titans, known to the Romans as Saturnus and full of mileage for bluffers. He presided over the Golden Age, 'ho epi Kronou bios' in Greek or 'Saturnia regna' in Latin. Kronos swallowed his children as they were born in case one might overthrow him. His wife, Rhea, deceived him with the youngest, Zeus, by handing Kronos a swaddled stone instead. This is an example of the enduring relevance of the Classics. Men should not trust women; equally, they should look more carefully at what they're given.

You should certainly side with the Titans in general and Kronos in particular. Use them to berate all modern vulgarisms like the Olympics, equality, and pop music. For example, "The rot set in when the Titans were overthrown, you know."

Mercury

Or Hermes to the Greeks was the God of trading and thieves, nowadays to be found at the Stock Exchange. His Greek name is from 'herma', the demon who haunts a pile of stones, and that's the most exciting thing you can say about him. He invented the lyre and stole Apollo's cattle.

Because they couldn't think of any more non-executive directorships to give him and because he was bone idle, the other Gods made him run errands for them to the corner shop for fags and things like that.

Pan

Like Bacchus, Pan is a first-rate chap, even though his father was Hermes and his mother unknown. He spent his time making flocks fertile; perhaps that is why he is half man, half goat and very promiscuous or, as a bluffer would say, amorous. Not a good man to cross – the nymph Echo refused his advances so he drove some shepherds mad and they tore her to pieces. Classicists describe this as 'the bucolic idyll'.

Persephone

Quite a girl, this. You should respect and, possibly, idealise her because her life-story tells you everything you need to know about living and dying. You won't even hear one like it in a bar in Dublin. Good literature, and art in general, is full of her.

Mention, casually, Goethe's Proserpina of the mid-1770s, Schiller's *Complaint of Ceres alias Demeter* and Shelley's *Song of Proserpine*. Even Stravinsky's 1934 opera *Persephone* is about her, or so some critics think, when they do.

Persephone was reluctantly married to **Hades** (Roman alias Pluto), God of the Underworld, when he forcibly carried her off, or rather down, whereupon the Earth went infertile in protest. Her mother, Demeter, sought help from an Industrial Tribunal and was eventually allowed to have her upstairs for a third of the year, whereupon the Earth went on to work to rule.

Zeus

A complete fake, he created neither Gods nor men and owes his fame to Homer, who must have been after a knighthood. Then **Aeschylus** got hold of him, made him Righteous and Just and generally did for him what spin doctors now do for politicians. You, however, are not fooled.

Zeus made himself Chief God without Portfolio so that, in practice, he was free to get on with his only obvious interest, fornication. This he did with considerable aplomb, swallowing the mistresses he got tired of, if Hera hadn't already dealt with them. He epitomised the Renaissance man, equally comfortable in the sheets with Gods, Demi-Gods, boys, girls and mortal women.

His speciality was disguises. Admire Michelangelo's (1475-1564) marvellous drawing of Leda and the swan, alias Zeus, and trot out Graham Hough's lines which just about cover the subject:

'Ageless, lusty, he twists into bull, ram, serpent,
Swan, gold rain; a hundred wily disguises
To catch girl, nymph or goddess; begets tall heroes
Monsters, deities . . . All that scribe or sculptor
Chronicles is no more than fruit of his hot embraces
With how many surprised recumbent breasts and haunches.'

Demi-Gods

Achilles
Too hackneyed to interest a good bluffer, you should wear a confident smirk of disdain when anyone is banal enough to mention him. If pressed for a view, say: "What would you expect of a man forced to spend his formative years as a girl?"

Aeneas
A son of Aphrodite, the sort of solid, decent chap that the Victorians admired but you don't. You have no time for a man whose epithet was 'pius' (pious). Escaping from burning Troy with his father on his shoulders, he wandered about a bit, ditched Dido, entered the Underworld, agonised endlessly about his Destiny, eventually stole some land from its natives and founded NOT Rome but Lavinium.

Cassandra   (B)
Rewards serious study as the epitome of the fatalistic eschatology that characterises the Classical world. A good quote here is 'To die is good, but not to be born is best' (Sophocles – but he probably whipped it from

Greek lyric poetry, either Archilochus or Mimmermus or Alcaeus or someone like that).

Apollo wanted to bed Cassandra and showered her with gifts, including that of prophecy. When she refused the casting couch, he added the sort of clause to her contract that you now find in holiday insurance. She would always prophesy truly, but no-one would believe her (as in the case of the Trojan Horse). Use her for such lines as: "Although I foretold the collapse of Communism, I was treated as a Cassandra."

Herakles

Hercules to the Romans, but never to you, is a (great bluffer's word) 'theophoric' name, in this case 'Hera's Glory'. Hera had a thing about him because, surprise, surprise, he was one of Zeus' innumerable bastards. She tried to kill him at birth with serpents (which he strangled) and 12 impossible labours (which you will refer to as 'The Athloi'). More recondite and, therefore, better bluffs to be had from reference to Herakles' 'Parerga' and 'Praxeis', the things he got up to when he wasn't working as a stable boy.

Try the Parergon (that's singular) of the ape-like Kerkopes. They tried to steal Herakles' weapons, so he hung them upside-down from a pole across his shoulders, thereby affording them an unparalleled view of his genitalia. So ribald were the resulting jokes that Herakles let them go. "What", you will ask, "does this tell us about proto-narcissism in the Niebelungenlied?"

Having said that or, as you would say, 'Quo dicto', you must know and bluff for hours about Herakles' Labour of entering Hades (Hell) to get hold of a Fair Lady, Alcestis, and return her to her beloved Admetus. You will either regard this tale as the proto-type of fetishism or expound upon its dominating dominance in Western art. It depends on what sort of parties you go to.

Prometheus

A Titan and thundering good chap, except that he didn't make any money out of it. By stealing fire from heaven and bringing it to earth, he stuck up for homo sapiens when Zeus wanted to blow all of us away.

The penalties for this action were both general and particular. Zeus punished us all by creating woman, the first of whom, Pandora, let all the evils that now afflict us out of the box she had been told to keep shut. Prometheus he punished by chaining him to a rock and arranging to have an eagle/vulture gnaw by day at his liver, which regenerated itself by night. This is the first recorded instance of ecology, yet one strangely ignored by Friends of the Earth.

When Hermes came to deliver a message from Zeus, Prometheus showed enormous fortitude and replied: 'I would not exchange my misery for your servitude.' No wonder Tertullian saw the crucified Christ as the 'true Prometheus'. Ficino (obiit 1499) treated him as the microcosm of man at his fullest development (you approve), but Ronsard (obiit 1585) saw him as a disguise for the sin of Adam (you disapprove).

You will admire Goethe's play about him (1773), agree with Francis Bacon that his story 'demonstrateth and presseth many grave and true speculations', ignore Shelley's drama *Prometheus Unbound*, if only because it was written in Italy, and master some really bad and obscure poetry about him by Longfellow:

'Ah, Prometheus! Heaven-scaling!
In such hours of exultation
Even the faintest heart, unquailing,
Might behold the vulture sailing
Round the cloudy crags Caucasian.'

Bluffers should make much of the 'Promethean qualities' of Orwell's Winston, Ivan Denisovich – and hen-pecked husbands.

Romulus and Remus

Said to have founded Rome, but you know it wasn't built in a day. They were suckled by a she-wolf, depicted by Turino's (Giovanni di, 1459) famous sculpture outside the Palazzo Pubblico in Siena, unless it's been sold since. Quote Macaulay's poem:

'The ravening she-wolf knew them
And licked them o'er and o'er
And gave them of her own fierce milk,
Rich with raw flesh and gore.'

Perhaps Longfellow isn't so bad after all.

Men (in the generic sense, of course)

You can approach this subject in one of two ways, either realistically or iconoclastically. The former involves knowing about the Dorians who invaded Greece from the north around 1100 BC and always thought they were superior to the Ionians and the Romans whose progenitors are very obscure, some of whom being cremators and others inhumators, and all that sort of thing – you will tire rapidly.

Hold, then, to the iconoclastic approach. Concentrate on who and what these people were, rather than whence they did or did not come. Praise, for example, the men of a Greek century – Aeschylus, Sophocles, Plato, Socrates, Pericles, Isocrates, Protagoras, Pheidias, Xenophon – and compare these with the products of a more recent century – Goethe, Shelley, Wordsworth, Beethoven, Schubert, Coleridge. Make two observations:

I. The Greek list is drawn from Athens, a polis whose population probably never exceeded 200,000. A comparable modern list must draw on many nations, even Germany.

II. With the exception of Socrates, everyone on the Greek list lived longer than anyone on the modern list. Sophocles began his magnificent play *Oedipus Coloneus* aged 90. King Agesilaus of Sparta was still active on the battlefield at 80. The longevity of the ancients was occasioned, you will assert, by the fact that, even in the Roman Republic, a typical meal consisted of two courses, the first a kind of porridge and the second, a kind of porridge. If only Byron had eaten more bran.

Aeschylus (525-456 BC)

The terror of generations of schoolboys who had to learn chunks of his plays by heart, you should concentrate on the 'hapax legomena' with which his plays are full. These are words which appear only once in (extant) Greek literature, made up by Aeschylus to prove how clever he was and to provide material for obscure PhDs.

You should mistrust someone who claims to understand Aeschylus' *Agamemnon* as much as you mistrust those who claim to have read James Joyce's *Finnegan's Wake*. Aeschylus was also the author of such perverted works as *The Oresteia* which gave us Freud and Guilt and were correctly described by Swinburne as 'the greatest spiritual work of man', although Aeschylus himself thought his work mere 'slices from Homer's banquet'.

Refer to Aristophanes' pastiche of Aeschylus' style in the *Frogs* ('Ranae' to you). Aristophanes didn't understand him either.

Aeschylus won the dramatic festivals (the Greek equivalent of an Oscar) so often that there were moves to ban him from entering. You should know that, whenever they lack the wherewithal with which to pay the Council Tax, modern authors whip something from Aeschylus. Faulkner's great labyrinths of error are Aeschylean and Eugene O'Neill's *Mourning Becomes Electra* (1931) goes on for hours about the moral dilemmas which Aeschylus covered in minutes. Eliot's *Murder in the Cathedral* (1935) is a rehash of the *Agamemnon* whilst Sartre's 1943 play, *Les Mouches*, does not contain a thing that isn't covered in Aeschylus.

Fortunately for those who struggle to understand the ancient Greek language, most of Aeschylus' plays have not survived. You might want to support Aeschylus because he wrote a play about Prometheus, but in general, and if only because Aristotle liked him, you should not.

Alexander (the Great) (356-323 BC)
Bluffers should pay Alexander special attention, since anyone who survived the tutorship of Aristotle must be all right. Concentrate on recondite facts: he was Alexander III, a man, a Macedonian (like coming from Leeds), fought and then fled his father Philip when they both wanted the same woman, was possibly a patricide, certainly a megalomaniac and probably insane.

With 91 of his Companions, he married an Iranian, murdered his best friend Kleitus, believed in World Domination and asked the Greeks to make him a God. Agree, reluctantly, that he was a hell of a good general and, perhaps, the most remarkable man ever to have lived.

Aristophanes (457-385 BC)
You will score points by asking anyone who refers to 'Aristophanes' whether they mean this one, of Athens, comic playwright, or Aristophanes of Byzantium (257-180 BC), scholar and polymath, successor to Eratosthenes as Supremo of the great library of Alexandria (before Caesar burnt it down). The 'Do you mean?' technique

is invaluable if someone asks you about an ancient of whom you know nothing. (See **Zenas of Sardis**.) As a bluffer, you will never doubt, for you will always imagine. Where there is ignorance, you will place fantasy.

That Aristophanes attempted to define the rules of Greek declension and began the controversy between Analogists and Anomalists which is still hotly debated in Oxbridge Senior Common Rooms when the dons feel that they must address themselves to issues of burning contemporary significance.

This Aristophanes is the one who wrote at least 42 plays of which 11 have survived. They are very funny, bawdy and bitterly satirical. Instance, in particular, Aristophanes' *Lysistrata* in which the wives of all the Greek states go on a sex-strike and thereby compel their warring husbands to make peace in order to make love. Similarly, in the *Ecclesiazusae* Aristophanes has the women of Athens take over the running of the city. They introduce community of property, make the men do the washing up and generally give us food for thought.

Aristophanes was very rude about all the great men of his time. They were not amused. In the *Clouds*, for example, he has Socrates running a 'Logic Factory' where the students are taught how not to pay their debts and debate whether gnats buzz through their mouths or their backsides as Socrates hangs in a basket 'gazing open-mouthed at the moving moon when a lizard pissed down on to him'. However Aristophanes survived the hostility of those he satirised, as well as two oligarchic revolutions and two democratic restorations. The *Spitting Image* team has nothing to worry about.

Having nothing better to do, Classical scholars have dreamt up the delineations of Old, Middle and New comedy. Both Old and Middle comedy are represented in Aristophanes' work (the 'Aristophanic corpus' to you), which just goes to show how bogus such categorisations are. You might wish to specialise in Middle comedy, since none has survived other than Aristophanes' plays that might not be Old and aren't New. Stock figures are courtesans, parasites, prostitutes and pimps.

Maintain that all comedy, Old, Middle, New (Menander, 342-289 BC), Roman (Plautus, 250-184 BC and Terence, 190-159 BC), Medieval, Molière, Sheridan, Shakespeare, Stoppard, is all but a poor derivative of the one and only Aristophanes, the only comic who has ever made you laugh.

Augustus (AD 63 BC-14)
Another megalomaniac, his two changes of name represent the first recorded attempt to fox the tax man. Born Gaius Octavius Thurinus, he became Gaius Julius Caesar Octavianus and then Augustus. He was also known, when it suited him, as Imperator (general) Caesar.

He didn't ask to be declared a God, but simply made himself one. When he wasn't murdering people he didn't like, his wife Livia was. Agrippa won his battles, but he took the credit. His memoirs, the *Res Gestae* (Things Done) are proof that Augustus was an imaginative man. He is said to be much admired by certain contemporary politicians, the Adam Smith Institute and Saddam Hussein.

Caesar (100-44 BC)
You should on no account stoop to discussing a man who made so great a reputation from so little and who was capable of saying of himself 'Satis diu vel naturae vixi vel gloriae', let alone 'Veni, vidi, vici'. You will maintain that the only arguably worthwhile thing he did was give us, on 1 January 45 BC, the Julian calendar and the 365-day year. You, however, will prefer

the Gregorian calendar or, better still, use 'AUC' which stands for 'ab urbe condita', from the founding of the city which was, of course, Rome. Thus 'such and such happened 100 years AUC'. This allows wonderful bluff, since no-one knows when Rome was founded.

In short, Caesar epitomises the bluffer's gentle art. Digress. Confound and confuse to impress. Discourse upon the recondite, and not upon Caesar's crossing of the Rubicon. Try "Roman concepts of spatio-temporal identity". They must have been pretty confused, with or without the Julian calendar. Quote a graffito from Pompeii which gives, or tries to give, a date: 'In the consulship of Nero Caesar Augustus and Cossus Lentulus, eight days before the Ides of February, on Sunday, on the sixteenth day of the moon, market-day at Cumae, five days before market-day at Pompeii.' Phew.

Caligula (AD 12-41)
You should say "Do you mean Gaius?" for Caligula (i.e. 'Baby Boots') was the nickname he earned by wearing military boots called 'caligae', his only inoffensive propensity. He became Emperor by changing Tiberius' will, but his habits of incest, sodomy, sadism and murder were too much, even for the Romans.

Callimachus (305-204 BC) (B)
You must know about his 7,000 line poem, the *Aetia* (Causes), and make much of it as the epitome of perfect poetry. Do so in the knowledge that, since only tiny fragments of it have survived, no-one can contradict you. Memorise and exploit the line 'Toe mega biblion ison toe megaloe kakoe' (A big book is a big evil), and thereby dismiss the *Satanic Verses*. Essential bluffers' words for the Callimachean creed are 'leptotes' (slenderness) and 'techne' (art).

Caracalla (AD 176-217)   (B)
Refer to him when anyone talks of the excesses of
Nero. Caracalla is less well-known and much, much
more excessive. You will undoubtedly impress.

Born Bassianus, he adopted the name Alemannicus
after he had exterminated, for fun, an obscure and
harmless tribe called the Alemanni. Meanwhile, he
was really called Marcus Aurelius Antoninus but pre-
ferred Caracalla, from the long, hooded, Gaulish
cloaks he liked to wear, like Dr Death.

He actually inherited the throne jointly with his
brother, Geta, but murdered him before proceeding to
have 20,000 male and 20,000 female supporters of
Geta disembowelled, emasculated, crucified, quartered
and generally made dead. Caracalla extended Roman
citizenship to all free inhabitants of the Roman
Empire, but people soon found out why – at a stroke,
Caracalla had trebled his tax base. Adding to this the
innovation of Inheritance Tax at 10 per cent, he was
able to spend and murder on an unprecedented scale.

Claim to enjoy the irony of the concerts and cultural
extravaganzas now performed in Rome's great Baths
of Caracalla, the audiences thinking of the Grandeur
that was Rome and all that stuff. Caracalla did a lot
in his Baths, but you know that none of it could ever
be described as cultural.

Catiline (?-62 BC)   (B)
Underrated and a bluffer's must, or 'sine qua non', as
you should say, he championed the poor and discon-
tented, especially dissolute aristocrats and bankrupt
Sullan veterans. **Cicero** harangued him for years
(one of his more interminable speeches is the *In
Catalinam*) and eventually had him and his army of
weirdos killed as they marched on Rome. Oppose the
view that Catiline was an anarchist. He just didn't
like Cicero, and who can blame him?

Victorian Classicists regarded him as a cross between Holmes' Moriarty and Batman's Penguin: 'Swept away in the eddy of the universal immorality, in early youth Catiline flung himself into all possible pleasures and excesses which, without undermining his gigantic strength, blunted his moral feelings and led him into a chain of awful crimes, through which his name stands out in history as one of the monsters of mankind.' You, however, know better.

Catullus (87-54 BC)
A rake and first-rate poet, usually in metres like phalaecian hendecasyllabics or scazons, but there are examples of pure iambics, glyconics, asclepiadeans and priapeans, especially in his smutty glyconic epithalamia (wedding poems, but no-one else will know either). You get the general idea.

Catullus was a member of the Roman equivalent of the Bloomsbury Group, a group of poets and dandies called the 'Neoterics' and disliked by Cicero. They wrote poems of remarkable skill and obscenity.

Cicero (106 BC ad nauseam)
Wrote and, worse still, published endless speeches without main verbs and even more tedious philosophical works like the *De Natura Deorum* which he lifted, unashamedly and almost verbatim, from the Greeks. He had an amanuensis, called Tyro, which sounds sore but was a secretary.

A natural Democrat, he described the people of Rome as 'faex Romana' (the faeces of Rome). The only other time he said anything brief was when he came out into the Forum to tell the plebs what had happened to the supporters of Catiline. 'Vixerunt,' he said – They have lived.

Diogenes the Cynic (412-323 BC) (B)
When asked what was the right time to marry,
Diogenes replied: 'For a young man, not yet. For an
old man, never.' Anticipating the jet-set, he shuttled
between Athens and Corinth in order to enjoy the
mild winters of the one and the cool summer breezes
of the other. He insisted that he was, thereby, better
off than the King of Persia, who had to travel great
distances to achieve the same results.

You should correct, peremptorily, anyone who, in
their ignorance, uses the term 'cynic' pejoratively.
Quote the definitive Cynic himself: 'Happiness con-
sists in but one thing, that a man truly enjoy himself
and never be grieved, in whatever place or circumstances he finds himself.' He thought that the wise
man 'regards the sense-organs given him by nature
as gods and uses them rightly . . . getting pleasure
from hearing and seeing, from food and from sex.'
Who would disagree with that?

Draco (floruit = was going strong, 620 BC)
Established a set of laws for Athens. When asked why
he specified death as the penalty for most offences, he
replied that small offences deserved death and he
knew of no severer penalty for great ones.

Eubulides of Miletus (floruit 3rd century BC) (B)
A philosopher, he didn't like Aristotle. He devised
ingenious paradoxes like 'the Liar' which have baffled
logicians, including German ones, ever since. If a man
says 'I am lying', is he telling the truth?

In its original form, Epimenides the Cretan says:
'All Cretans are liars.' If he is telling the truth, he is
lying; if he is lying, he is telling the truth. Its
medieval formulation was:
Socrates: 'What Plato is about to say is false.'
Plato: 'Socrates has just spoken truly.'

You will, of course, digress from here and bring in Kant, Pythagoras, Darwin and anyone else you can think of, whilst always coming back to Eubulides' *Paradox of Definition*, otherwise known as the Sophism of the Slippery Slope. For example:

a) Protagoras: a young lawyer had an agreement with his teacher, Protagoras. If he won his first case, he would pay for his instruction; if he lost, he would not. He kept refusing to accept cases until Protagoras sued him. Naturally, the young lawyer defended himself. If he lost he would not pay and if he won he would not pay.

b) Darwin: 'The survival of the fittest'. The fittest cannot be the strongest nor the cleverest – weakness and stupidity survive everywhere. The only way of determining fitness, then, is that a thing does survive. 'Fitness' is 'survival'. Darwinism: 'Survivors survive'.

There are hours and hours of wonderful bluff here. Bring in any paradoxical story you know. Attribute them all to Eubulides. Sprinkle your conversation with oxymorons (compressed paradoxes) like 'loud silence', 'living death'. Say that your harvest is the forest which you did not plant. Plant sequoias. Invest in the millennium. Practise resurrection.

Heraklitus (floruit 500 BC) (B)
An admirably arrogant philosopher (beloved of 'I am the master of this college/What I don't know isn't knowledge' Jowett, Master of Balliol College, Oxford). A typical Heraklitan observation is: 'Other men do not notice what they do when they are awake, just as they forget what they do when asleep.' Essential for bluffers are some of his cryptic sayings: 'Everything flows', 'The road up and down is the same.' Take on

Haiku bluffers any day with Heraklitus.

Herodotus (484-420 BC)

Adopt a strong line. Reject Cicero's view of him as the 'father of history'. State that he was a mendacious and provincial geographer, logographer and mythographer, never a historian. Your point is that he never spoilt a story for want of a few facts. Clinch the argument by quoting Juvenal: Et quidquid Graecia mendax audet in historia' (Whatever else the lying Greek dares in his history). Be confident; anyone who excites so much interest amongst German Classicists as Herodotus must be deeply suspect.

Hesiod (floruit 8th century BC)

If someone claims that Homer is the earliest Greek poet, you will claim that Hesiod was, and vice-versa. Krafft is your man here: his opus *Vergleichende Untersuchungen zu Homer und Hesiod* is both original and good. But the part that is original is not good and the part that is good is not original.

Even the Greeks didn't know which was the earlier of the two poets. Ancient scholars devoted their lives to this utterly fatuous question. That modern scholars do likewise is further proof, to you, of continuity in the Classics.

You will know that Hesiod wrote the *Works and Days* (which urges everybody to be thrifty, industrious and interminably dull) and the *Theogony* (a list of who slept with whom and when on Mount Olympus, a sort of 8th-century *Dallas*). Don't linger too long on these two. For some reason many people have read or at least know of these works. Your bluff, instead, will be: "Did Hesiod write, or did he not, the *Aspis* (Shield), the *Catalogue of Women,* the *Astronomia,* and other lost works?" You know that you don't know. But you know that your audience doesn't know, either.

Homer (? c.1800-200 BC)

Although illiterate and blind, he wrote the *Iliad* and
Odyssey. This is the sort of salient probability in
which the Classics abound. So you may as well
attribute other stray epics to him – the *Cypria*, the
Thebais, the *Homeric Hymns* and, if you're very good,
the *Epigoni*. The crux of his style is to repeat the
same old line (called a formula) when you don't know
what else to say. It was his version of the politician's
stutter. Thus, every morning, and there are a lot of
mornings in Homer, we have: 'As soon as primal
Dawn first touched the sky with her fingers of pink
light'. What a line, though.

Homer's other trick is the 'epithet'. Agamemnon is
always 'anax andron' (lord of men), Odysseus always
'polymetis' (many-counselled) and Zeus, of course, is
always ready. It's great padding. You will disparage,
comparatively and utterly, today's revolting equivalent, the ubiquitous 'situation', as in 'not an on-going
options situation', a 'confrontation situation', even (in
rugby commentaries) a 'ruck situation'.

You believe that if people have nothing worthwhile
to say, the very least they can do is to shut up. You
are amused by a modern age in which, for all its
emphasis on speed, the inhabitants are unable to
communicate even their own confusion. From formu-
laic, epithetical Homer we are a but sorry declension.

This is the sort of digression in which you must
excel. It contains the long-suffering, much-enduring,
far-seeing, all-knowing fortitude that is the desired
image of every Classical bluffer. But if you're off
colour, go for the Oral Tradition instead. Homer
passed from mouth to mouth, and it is quite something to be able to recite a 16,000-line poem or two.
Nowadays, people have to watch the 11 o'clock news
to remind themselves of what was on the 9 o'clock
news.

You can mention, in passing, Radermacher's view that Homer was a pacifist because, in the *Iliad*, Zeus doesn't like Ares. You should also know about Zoilus Homeromastix, 'Scourge of Homer' who, even in 330 BC, thought that Homer was a fibber.

Nonetheless, maintain with reverence that whoever Homer was, if he ever was, he was author of some of the most remarkable poetry known to man. Memorise and quote, often, such lines as:

> '. . . men who are as leaves are, and now flourish and grow warm with life, and feed on what the ground gives, but then again fade away and are dead.'
>
> — *Iliad* XXI. 464-6.

Declare that you find in Homer a haunting tension between delight in life and acceptance of its unalterable framework. You admire and emulate this – enormously.

You read only Lattimore's translation of the *Iliad* and Fitzgerald's of the *Odyssey*.

Horace (65-8 BC)

The Sir John Betjeman of his day, he has supplied more quotes to the cognoscenti than the rest of Latin literature put together. He began a long and distinguished tradition by taking up the pen because he was skint. In return for eulogising Augustus, he got a bursary for life and a farm in the Sabine Hills. The Arts Council can't compete. You will bemoan the passing of patronage.

He was a modest sort of chap: 'Exegi monumentum aere perennius ... non omnis moriar' – I have made a monument more lasting than bronze ... I shall not wholly die...' (*Odes, Liber* III.30) and wrote things like the *Carmen Saeculare*, a choral lyric in Sapphic metre to be performed by a choir of 27 boys and 27 girls.

Your best tack with Horace is to claim, with some justification, that he pinched all his best stuff from the Greeks, adding to it a certain smarminess that was entirely his own: 'Vixere fortes ante Agamemnona multi' – Many brave men lived before Agamemnon (*Odes*, IV.9.25-6). A good quote, that.

Juvenal (AD 55-140)

His 16 brilliant *Satires* are essential reading and range from the exposure of some very perverted vices to the extravagance of the ruling classes, the misery of poverty and hatred of Jews and women. Those who find today's inner-city life intolerable should read *Satire* III and realise that some things don't change.

Dryden's (1631-1700) versions of five of the *Satires* are his best work. *Satire* X is the model for Johnson's (1709-84) *Vanity of Human Wishes*. You are almost certain to be able to impress by knowing that the great question posed by liberal politicians and former intelligence officers – 'Who will guard the guardians?' – is from Juvenal (*Satire* VI (Oxon.).31-2). You must quote it in the Latin – 'Quis custodiet ipsos custodes?' – and bluff for several minutes about the importance of the 'ipsos' (themselves) in the original.

Lucretius (99-55 BC)

State that only Lucretius and Virgil were able to take a Greek model and make something greater of it. This may not be strictly true, but is, at least, distinctly controversial. Lucretius wrote a didactic epic in hexameters, the *De Rerum Natura* (Concerning the nature of the universe) which, unashamedly, regurgitates the atomic theories of the Greek philosophers Democritus (floruit 5th century BC) and Epicurus (341-270 BC).

Yet Lucretius writes poetry of a searing power and pathos. You do not know its equal. For example:

'... medio de fonte leporum
surgit amari aliquid quod in ipsis floribus angat'

'From the very heart of the fountain of delights, in pleasure's very flowers, there arises something bitter which
wounds.'   *DRN* IV.1133-4.

This is true. It is commonly experienced as a hang-
over, whilst everyone knows that 'post coitum, omnia
animalia tristia sunt'.

Nero (AD 37-68)
A vicious ancestry and depraved childhood made him
a natural Roman Emperor, arsonist and murderer of
his mother, sundry wives, Christians, Stoics, donkeys
and, eventually, himself.

Ovid (AD 43 BC-17)
He wrote, inter alia, an incredibly funny, bawdy but
also practical version of the Kama Sutra, the *Ars
Amatoria* (The Art of Loving), which is worth reading.
Augustus didn't like it much and banned Ovid to the
Black Sea where he wrote his *Tristia* (Sad Things). He
was really rated, however, for his *Metamorphoses*, an
idea lifted from various Greek poets, Nicander,
Parthenius and Callimachus. Because the Renaissance
and the Elizabethan Age thought it was original, they
made a lot of what you must call 'the Met'.

Arthur Golding translated the tales in 1565.
Poussin painted nothing else from 1629-1642. It was
the Germans, however, who got really excited. Goethe
had plants metamorphosing in 1798 and then animals
in 1806. By 1914, Rilke could think of nothing but
metamorphosis – Wandlung, Verwandlung, Wendung.
You do not think that Ovid would approve.

Pindar (518-438 BC)
Almost untranslatable, usually unintelligible and
always inexplicable, he is unfortunately the greatest
of Greek lyric poets.

Plato (429-347 BC)

He nicked all his best ideas from Socrates but, to cover himself, passed them off as Socrates'. Maybe he was Socrates. He believed in Forms and disliked women and democracy, whilst he was wrong about tyranny. According to his Theory of Forms, an elephant is both large and small – a small elephant, a large animal. Hitting someone is good and bad – good when it is just, bad when it is not. This all goes to prove that no-one with a mental age over four can be a philosopher, let alone a philosopher king (Plato's version of a tyrant). If he was bad, the Neo-Platonists like Plotinus (AD 205-270) were even worse.

Bluffers who enjoy being economical with the truth will revel in Plato's *Republic*: 'If anyone at all is to have the privilege of lying, the rulers of the state should be the persons and they ... may be allowed to lie for the public good.' (Book III.389). You will move from there, of course, to Juvenal (Quis custodiet...) and then to Eubulides (of the Slippery Slope) and then back to a Demosthenic oration on contemporary politics.

Pyrrhus (319-272 BC)

Easily the most famous of the Molossian Kings of Epirus he followed the fortunes of Demetrius the Besieger and conquered Parauaea, Tymphaea, Ambracia, Amphilochia and Acarnania before inheriting Corcyra and Leucas by marrying the daughter of Agathocles and then the daughter of the Dardanian Bardylis but only when his first wife Antigone was dead.

You must deliver this with a breathless intensity. Pyrrhus even defeated the Romans (once) at Heraclea in 280 with 25,000 men and 20 elephants. He won the battle but lost his army, hence the phrase 'Pyrrhic victory'.

Pythagoras (floruit 550 BC)
Pinched his theorem from Babylon and then sacrificed an ox because he was a vegetarian. Played with ducks in his bath. Equated abstractions with numbers: Justice = 4; Happiness = 0. Never actually wrote a word and his followers were sworn to secrecy, but we are still absolutely certain that he believed in metempsychosis.

Sappho (floruit 600 BC)
Was a Lesbian not because she was a lesbian, but because she lived on Lesbos, the island where she ran a Greek version of a Swiss finishing school, except that hers honoured Aphrodite and the Muses, not Manners and Money. She still found the time to marry Kerkylas and have a child called Kleis. Otherwise, she was kept busy writing quite astonishingly good poetry and you will maintain that she is the finest ever poet of the feminine gender.

Alas, only two of her odes and mere fragments of her work survive. If you have read them, your bluff is complete. If you haven't, make use of:

i) the vicissitudes of the manuscript tradition, the burning of the Alexandrian library, the perishability of papyrus.

ii) an exposition on other female poets of antiquity, Corinna, Praxilla, even a Roman, Sulpicia; the indomitability of the female spirit and so on.

The first is best: try a fragment of Fragment 199 (*LGS*) in Lattimore's splendid translation:

'Like the very gods in my sight is he who sits where he can look in your eyes, who listens close to you, to hear the soft voice, its sweetness murmur in love and laughter, all for him. But it breaks my spirit; underneath my breast all the heart is shaken.'

Every good bluffer will know how she feels.

Socrates (469-399 BC)
A good bluffer will simply say "Do you mean Plato?",
but use Socrates' technique of elenchus to confuse
yourself and others. At its simplest, make others define
Justice, Truth, Virtue, Happiness and so on and, when
they come up with something, keep asking "Why?"

Themistocles (528-462 BC)
Athenian politician and 'strategos' which was a general but he actually commanded the Athenian fleet.

You can relate a few good tales about Themistocles.
With the Persians pressing hard in 480 BC, the
Greeks had to decide whether to fight the Persian
fleet at Salamis or withdraw their fleet to the
Isthmus. Themistocles persuaded the commander-in-
chief to debate the matter, but started to speak before
the motion was formally put to the meeting.
'Themistocles,' said a Corinthian, 'in the games those
who start too soon are whipped'. 'And those who start
too late,' was the retort, 'win no prizes'. At another
amicable meeting, Themistocles was told to shut up
or be struck. 'Strike!' he said, 'but hear me!'

Thucydides (460-400 BC)
By means of making up speeches in his *History* for
the people who made up the war in which they say
what he thought they thought they did or ought to,
might have, could have done, thereby explaining,
commenting, elucidating and rationalising in accord
with a History written not for the applause of the
moment but for all time and resting on what he himself saw and on the reports of others, after careful
research aiming at the greatest possible accuracy in
each case, he wrote a history of and, to a large extent,
created the Peloponnesian War.

His prose is usually every bit as tortuous as that sentence. Quote Quintilian: Thucydides' style is 'densus et fusus et semper instans sibi' (constipated and indigestible and always standing on its own toes). For all that, the product of it is essential reading for any bluffer, and especially Pericles' Funeral Speech (Book II. 35-46), especially in translation.

Virgil (70-19 BC)   (BB)
He wrote splendid advertising copy for Augustus, every bit as perfidious as 'Things go better with Coke'. You simply MUST, nonetheless, master a few choice Virgilian quotes. They might even help you on your next outing to Tuscany. Try:

'Mens immota manet, lacrimae volvuntur inanes.'
His will remained unmoved, in vain fall his tears.
    — *Aeneid* IV.449. For the bank manager's 'No'.

'Ibant obscuri sola sub nocte per umbram.'
In gloom they passed through the shadows of unpeopled night.
    — *Aeneid* VI.628. For the Channel Tunnel.

'Sunt lacrimae rerum, et mentem mortalia tangunt.'
Literally, There are tears of things, and the affairs of mortal men touch the mind.
    — *Aeneid* I.463. How you feel when depressed.

Concentrate on Virgil as proof of the enduring validity of the Classics. You do know that he was a Roman (almost), but all his best stuff comes from Homer. Your scope for vintage bluff now makes its masterpiece. In the Middle Ages, grammar was learnt from Virgil and shaded into 'grammayre', a word for magic. So Virgil became a Great Magician and made a bronze fly to protect Naples against all other flies. He also balanced the city on an egg.

People opened his work ('opera' to you, and that's plural: if you're especially smooth, refer, instead, to the 'Virgilian corpus') and selected a line, blindfolded, as an omen. Walpole consulted Virgil on the character of George II and drew *Aeneid* III.620: 'You, Gods, drive such a monster from the earth.' Charles I, at the opening of the Civil War, drew upon Dido's curse on Aeneas (*Aeneid* IV.615ff and very strong stuff) and we know what happened to him.

The only time he proved that he was human, St Paul wept at Virgil's tomb and said (was he always so pompous?): 'What would I have made of you, had I found you alive?' The bluffer should ask an enthralled audience whether the Roman world was ready for Billy Graham.

The Renaissance produced innumerable Virgilian epics, from Petrarch's *Africa* to Fracastoro's *Syphilis* or 'The French Disease'. The first opera (as in music, and not as in the plural of 'opus'), Dante, Milton, Dryden, Pope, Tennyson, T.S. Eliot, Mussolini, Saatchi & Saatchi, all are derivatives of the great old Mantuan to whom all good bluffers should kneel.

Zenas of Sardis, Lusitania, Virunum, Patmos, Calomodunum, Surbiton (8th century BC – 2nd century AD)   (B)

Poet/Polymath/Pederast/Publican/Politician/Pimp/ Banker/Philosopher. Your 'deus ex machina' and 'sine qua non'. Be confident, authoritative, imaginative and, above all, mendacious. Every bluffer MUST have one. Even the Germans make them up.

WHAT?

You must maintain, inexorably and ineluctably, that there were only six constituents of the Classical Age:

I. Democracy

Most people believe that it is to the Classical world that we owe Democracy and her handmaidens, Peace, Brotherhood, the Common Agricultural Policy and the IMF. Bluffers know better.

Neither the Greeks nor the Romans knew anything about Democracy at all. Its only connection with the Classics is its etymology. The only occasion on which anything like it occurred in the Classical world was for 20-30 years in Athens and, apart from producing the Parthenon, that was a disaster. Even then the 'people' ('demos' to you), excluded women, foreigners, non-citizens and (especially) dogs. The fallacy of Democracy was invented by an exiled aristocrat, Thucydides, in the Periclean Funeral Oration (which he also made up). The Athenian 'democracy' was utterly stratified: it was not nice to be born a member of the lower orders, the Thetes or the Zeugitae. The chances were that you would end up rowing your life out in a trireme as some aristocrat beat a drum and cracked a whip.

'Democracy' was always in the hands of either aristocratic and unbelievably dense 'strategoi', or ill-bred demagogues who spent most of their time chewing garlic and drinking ouzo under olive trees. The Classical world flourished not under Democracy but under Tyranny. This contains a moral not entirely unnoticed by certain contemporary politicians.

II. Homosexuality

You should know, whatever your own proclivities, that the Greeks and Romans were definitely for it. Concentrate on the absence of literary epigrapha concerning lesbianism for you know that 'homosexual' is from the Greek 'homos' (like), and, technically, if not in the Callimachean sense, applies equally to women.

Express surprise that homo Classicus managed to reproduce himself at all; hint at Classical and precocious knowledge of artificial insemination. Such reference will make you seem something of a polymath, if not a polysexual.

You should know Alcaeus' odes to boys' bottoms and be familiar with Martial's epigrams: e.g., ix.67: 'I had a wanton mistress . . . Exhausted, then, I asked for something boyish.' You will quote Juvenal's advice to his readers: 'If you wish to shorten your life with sexual pleasure, take it with a boy, not a woman' (vi.33).

All sound stuff. Yet the distinguished bluffer, now and in perpetuam, (as in 'ave atque vale') will ask about this and any other subject's 'wider ramifications', in this case:

III. Misogyny

The original Greek Goddess was Gaia, the Earth-Mother, and the Romans were very keen on Vestal Virgins who were actually prostitutes and so, logically, the Classical world was run by misogynists for misogynists.

In his (vital bluffers' reading) *Satyricon*, Petronius gives the general idea: 'Some women are kindled to love by the dirt. Their passion is never aroused unless they see a slave in short garments. Others burn for a man from the arena or a mule-driver thick with dust' and so on.

The evidence is clear: Demosthenes, for example; 'Hetairai (Geisha girls) we keep for the sake of pleasure, concubines for the daily care of our persons, wives to bear us legitimate children and to be the trusted guardians of our households.' Aristotle argues in his *Politics* that by nature the male is superior, the female inferior, therefore the man rules and the woman is ruled.

IV. Slavery

The Greeks and Romans took a strong line, yes, especially in 'democratic' Athens. Aristotle described the correct 'modus vivendi' for a slave as 'work, punishment and food'. The Classical world got two out of three, which isn't bad; they forgot the food. Always a bit out of touch, Aristotle. For their part, the Romans had a proverb 'Quot servi, tot hostes' (Every slave is an enemy). They were right.

You should concentrate on the 'utopian nature' of the endless slave revolts of antiquity (Spartacus is essential), moving from there to Marx, the existentialist dilemma, the Diggers, the Luddites and the impending privatisation of the Police.

You will note, quizzically, that the slaves of antiquity didn't actually object to slavery per se; they just wanted to be free themselves.

Everybody thought the principle of slavery a sound one. Perhaps they were right. A Roman jurist said that by natural law all men are born free. He hastened to add that slavery existed by the law of nations. The Stoics taught that all men, including slaves, were brothers, but that man's welfare was purely spiritual and that slavery was no impediment to a man's being master of himself.

As that great Stoic philosopher and hypocrite

Seneca remarked (*Epistles* LXXX.9): 'When you buy a horse, you order its blanket to be removed; so, too, you pull the garments off a slave.'

The Christians were no better. St Paul told slaves not to worry about the condition to which they were called. When Christianity became the official religion, the Church did not advocate abolition but acquired slaves of its own. These days, the Moonies maintain the tradition.

V. Tyranny

You must defend tyranny, indeed extol it and correct those contemporary democrats who abuse it. Nothing that is anything in the Classical world would have come about without it. That Plato thought it the worst form of government is sufficient reason for you to praise it.

As often, the Classical world perfected it and we have messed it up. You should admire all tyrants except, perhaps, Pittacus of Mytilene, who imposed double fines for offences committed when drunk.

VI. Beauty

Lawrence Durrell had a Greek master at school who used to hold up a tattered photograph of the Venus de Milo, bang his fist on a desk and shout: 'What do you think they were trying to do? Make us tingle with lust? Certainly not! They were asking themselves what beauty is, and whether it lies in proportion.'

You will maintain that our age cannot even ask the right questions, let alone get the right answers. In their philosophy, their poetry, their great buildings, the Greeks sought and articulated the beautiful ('to kalon'), and even the Romans had the sense to stay on Greek tracks. Claim that there is no finer poetry than Pindar, no building more perfect than the Parthenon, no questions more acute than Socrates'. Meanwhile, the Association of Art Historians will continue to confer and declaim: 'A different perspective can propose that art has to be decentred from its nodal position for the imagery to be relocated within a nexus of interlocking circuits.' O tempora, O mores!

HOW?

How did they do it? By being tyrants, enslavers, misogynists, and never democrats, of course. Admit, however, that several other factors impinge:

I. Oracles, Omens and Auguries

Whenever a tyrant/enslaver/misogynist/non-democrat wanted to justify himself, he got an oracle/omen/augury to say that it was a good idea. Meaning nothing, they meant everything. Three examples will illustrate your point.

a) Croesus wasn't sure whether or not to cross the river Halys and attack Persia, so he asked the Delphic Oracle. When the Pythia replied that if he crossed the river he would destroy a mighty empire, Croesus crossed the river and did, indeed, destroy a mighty empire. Unfortunately, it was his own.

b) When the Persians seemed set to destroy Athens, the Delphic Oracle advised the Athenians to 'trust in your wooden walls'. Some thought this meant the wooden palisades which surrounded the

Acropolis of Athens: they were wrong. Others thought this meant the Athenian fleet: they were right, but that wasn't much comfort to those who were wiped out when the Persians captured and sacked the Acropolis, for all its wooden walls.

c) When the Roman admiral Manlius Vulso, or was it Attilius Regulus, desperately wanted to attack yet another Carthaginian fleet and get himself some fresh slaves, protocol demanded that he consult the sacred chickens crapping on his poop deck. If they ate the (sacred) wheat thrown to them, this was a good omen and he should attack. If they didn't, he shouldn't. When the chickens wouldn't touch the wheat, Manlius, or was it Attilius, simply had them thrown overboard, saying: 'If they will not eat, let them drink.' He lost the battle.

II. Armies

When they weren't killing their enemies, the Greeks and Romans thoroughly enjoyed killing each other and, whenever possible, they used armies. So they gave us phalanxes and Deputy Rear Air Vice Marshals and index-linked pensions and hoplites and legions and press gangs and Star Wars.

III. Oratory

The Greeks and Romans loved talking (and still do) and called it 'oratory'. The education of Achilles was entrusted to Phoenix, who was told to train Achilles to be a 'maker of speeches and a doer of deeds'.

When they weren't fighting, they made interminably long speeches to and about: each other, Democracy, Catiline, Freedom, Sex, the financing of

Local Government and other hardy perennials. Since the verb in both languages (except in Aeschylus and Cicero, who couldn't be bothered with main verbs at all) comes at the end of a sentence, they developed something called 'participles' and strung them together without conjunctions (called 'asyndeton') in interminable clauses (called 'clausulae') and so were able to speak for hours before anyone had a clue as to what they were saying.

Modern politicians, of course, do much the same thing, but badly. They are ignorant of ellipsis (the omission of words which can be supplied by their context) but they are big on pleonasm (the use of needless words, especially 'situation'). They have certainly discovered hyperbole (exaggeration) and periphrasis (the description of a fact by its attending circumstances), but litotes (saying less than is meant) and synecdoche (the part stands for the whole) are lost on them. Sic transit gloria mundi.

Demosthenes practised his speeches by putting a pebble in each cheek and declaiming to seagulls. His Philippics are famous for being purple. Cicero discovered the difference between 'oratio recta', which was painful, and 'oratio obliqua', which was incomprehensible.

IV. Ostracism

The Greeks developed ostracism and the Romans perfected it. Perhaps we should reintroduce it. This was a system of banishing unpopular individuals for ten years to places like Argos or the Black Sea. Citizens wrote the name of whoever they wanted to be rid of on potsherds called 'ostraka'. The Romans gave up the voting bit and just got on with the ostracism. Efficient lot, the Romans.

V. Art

The Greeks were good at art and the Romans good at copying it. Maintain that we can't do either. Argue that the strength and vibrancy of Greek art comes from its reconciliation of an antithesis: control on the one hand, passion on the other. Assert that the art of the ancients is so overwhelming precisely because it is so intelligently controlled.

You will only get away with such generalities for so long. To the particular: you will know that 'there is no one art in Classical Greece that is without its masterpieces'. Professor Boardman says so, and he isn't German. Most remarkable is that so much range and variety should have been produced by so few, be it in architecture, jewellery, sculpture, literature or monumental sarcophagi.

You will know the difference between Attic blackfigure and red-figure vases. The first are painted black, the second are not painted but 'reserved' on the pottery against a painted black background. Master recondite facts. The colossal bronze statue of Helios at Rhodes (the Colossus) was 33 yards high and toppled by an earthquake. More than a millennium later it took a train of 1,000 camels to carry off the scrap metal.

You will hear many say that the contribution of Rome to art was the arch. They are wrong. The Greeks knew all about it and, occasionally, used it, but generally avoided it for aesthetic reasons. The Romans gave us, instead concrete, for which you are not at all grateful.

You could do worse than specialise in the details of the orders: dentils, volutes, triglyphs, metopes, arrises, flutes and so on. A little knowledge allows you to prefer the Doric order, especially its finest expression, the Parthenon, which displays some Ionic elements, and perhaps be contemptuous of the Corinthian order, if only because Vitruvius (floruit 30 BC) says it was invented by a bronze-worker, Callimachus, who was inspired by the sight of an acanthus plant growing up around a basket.

Use 'Deinde cessavit ars' (Then art stopped). A good, identikit quote from the Roman scholar Pliny (AD 24-79), recording the course of Greek art after the achievements of the sculptor Lysippus (floruit 320 BC). Thus did Pliny consign to oblivion all those endless artists who toiled under the Hellenistic kings. He was right. So are you.

VI. Language and Metre

Greek, like its cousin, Latin, is a highly inflected language with an enormously elaborate and complex syntax. Many have discovered this, to their sorrow. It is in the nature of Greek to express with great precision things which by their nature are very imprecise and which most non-bluffers cannot express at all in any language. These are not only the relations between ideas but shades of meaning and emotion.

You can go a long way, however, by understanding that the key to Greek and, to a lesser extent, Latin, is the participle. The regular Greek verb (there are a few, though most are horribly irregular) has 10 participles and its Latin counterpart, three.

You will not find in Greek the woolliness into which English often deviates and from which German rarely emerges. The secret is to find the main verb (when there is one) and hang on in there, riding the labyrinths of clauses and participles and thought. A bit like surfing, really.

Metre, though, is quite another story and worthy of hours of splendid bluff. Begin by saying that the West is incapable of comprehending the 'quantitative verse' of the Greeks, Romans and the East, because our verse, by complete contrast, is 'stressed'. Then turn to the highly complex poetry of the Greeks where complex thoughts required complex metres, or was it the other way round.

Dactyls and iambs and cretics and trochees and spondees are pretty straightforward. It's when you get to your knowledge of dactylo-trochaic tetrapody catalectics or pherecratean glyconic hipponactean acatalectic telesilleia that you will impress and deserve your caesura (a break), be it penthemimeral (in the fifth foot) or even hephthemimeral (in the seventh foot: if you find one in a hexameter – a line of six feet – you've gone too far).

If all else fails, use epitrites, a term owed to the frequency of the sequence ‿ ‒‒, a ratio of 3:4, taking the length of a short (a 'breve' to you) as the standard. Then move on to the Golden Mean and the Delphic Oracle's Omphalos and 'Know Yourself' and Kierkegaard and Proust before returning, your strophic responsion, to the encomiologicum (‒‿‿ ‒‿‿ ‒ // ‿ ‒‒) and its related form the praxilleion (‒‿‿ ‒‿‿ ‒‿‿ ‿ ‒‒).

You will find this bluff especially useful for social events to which you wish never to be invited again.

VII. Thought

You will draw an important distinction here. The Greeks could and did think. The Romans couldn't and didn't and have, therefore, much in common with the present. The 'thought' of the Classical world which has shaped the West and formed the best of what we are is singularly, exclusively Greek. Maintain, categorically, that Rome produced no original thought or philosophy. You might even be right.

The Greeks, however, were always thinking, about justice, beauty, truth, God, mathematics, physics, architecture, medicine. When they ran out of other things to think about, they thought about thinking.

The subject of Greek 'thought' is one too difficult, vast and ponderous for a serious bluffer. Concentrate, instead, as an example of synecdoche (= the part for the whole), on the Greek concept of logos, one so laden with meaning that even the Greeks themselves had to think hard about it. You may bluff for hours on the subject, for no-one can fairly contradict you. Logos is, at once, both the word by which an inward thought is expressed and that inward thought itself. You will digress immediately to Chomsky and the science of semantics. The word also means 101 other things – account, calculation, condition, analogy, deliberation – when you can remember them.

Heraklitus was the first to use the word to signify the intelligible law of the universe. The Stoics, or perhaps even Zeno, beefed up this metaphysical meaning, pervading the whole of the natural world with 'orthos logos'. Digress at once to the Gospel of St John ('In the beginning was the Word.' 'En arche ain ho logos.'), the Dead Sea Scrolls, the cosmogony of Plato's *Timaeus* and the modification of the schools of Alexandria. Make such statements as: "Thus, you see, was a transcendental monotheism combined with an original pantheism."

Now reinforce your first point by repetition, arguing that, in essence, Greek thought was so brilliant because it probed and examined and questioned everything, including its right to question. Only in its teaching of mathematics, where the important thing is to ask the right questions, rather than to get the right answers, does the modern world come close to the Greek example. But then why should it? Why should it not? What is 'it'? What is 'is'? It's as easy as that.

WHY?

It is not good enough to reply 'Why not?' A trifle too Socratic. Every good bluffer must give this utterly fatuous question grave and dignified consideration. After all, many worthy people in obscure universities write interminable theses on 'The Spirit of the Classical Age and the Socio-Economic Problems of Albania' and so on.

These rambles contain, inter alia and when one can find a main verb or, indeed, any verb, diarrhoeal dissertations on the quest for 'Logos', 'Episteme', 'Arete', 'Virtus', 'Pietas' (and many other things which no-one will ever understand) seeking in these the substance of the Classics.

Assert that this is all utter twaddle: the Classical world continued so long as it understood that it couldn't understand anything; it produced some who grasped this truth and others who didn't or who, if they did, chose to pretend that they didn't and who, thereby, kept the show on the road: sybarites and sodomites and sadists and cynics and orgies and stoics and endless people asking 'Where are we going? Why are we going there? What is the Good?' and never reaching an answer.

When the Classical world finally admitted that it could not understand, it gave up and handed the baton to the Goths, Semi-Goths, Ostrogoths and Vandals. The Dark Ages allowed 'logos' some beauty sleep before the Renaissance, Classicism, Neoclassicism and German scholars stirred the whole thing up again. As Pindar says, 'Ti de tis, ti de oo tis; skias onar anthropos' – What is man, what is he not? Man is a shadow of a dream.

VITAL BLUFFERS' PHRASES

You must have a good stock of phrases to be used liberally and, ideally, incomprehensibly. You are pursuing the form, not the substance, and people will understand you especially when they don't. Never use an English phrase when a Classical bluff will do. Exempli gratia:

You haven't got a difficult job, it's Sisyphean; your dilemma is an elenchus; you live in Arcadia, not Gloucestershire; others solve problems, you cut Gordian knots; you have the wisdom of Solon, not Solomon, and prefer Archilochus to Eliot. Stoppard is Aristophanic and you are Promethean, not irreligious. Your designer togs are Koan, your wife Aspasian or your husband Kleisthenic.

You call your dog Cerberus and you love like Orpheus, preferring Sappho to Graves. Your boss is Damoclean and you read Democritus, not Brookner. Your cynicism is Diogenic and your world-view Hecataean. Your astronomy is Metonic and your body Polygnotan, rather than beautiful. You are never separated or divorced but 'a mensa et toro', from table and bed.

You avoid the vulgarity of signing your letters 'Yours sincerely'. Use 'Ex animo' instead. It means, literally, from the mind/spirit/soul, perhaps 'from the heart'. Similarly, everyone uses 'et cetera', although few can spell it and fewer still know that it means 'and other things' (neuter plural). 'k.t.l.' is much smoother. It stands for 'kai ta loipa', Greek for 'and the remaining things'.

You will also master, at least, the following:

Carthago delenda est – Carthage must be destroyed. 'I'll nail the bastard.'

Alea iacta est – The die is cast. 'The shit has hit the fan.'

Tabula rasa – The slate having been wiped clean.

What the banks do when they convert your meagre overdraft to a secured personal loan at an APR of 1,483,876 per cent.

Hapax legomena – Things once being said. 'One night stands.' Singular, legomenon.

Hominis est errare – To err is human. 'But you're still sacked'.

Odi profanum vulgus et arceo – I hate and shun the vulgar masses. 'I don't watch *Neighbours*/I have not been to Tenerife.'

Q.V. – 'Quo Vadis', whither are you going, the question the Classical world was unable to answer and we are unable even to ask, and the title of an astonishingly obscure Polish novel by Henryk Sienkiewicz, which won a Nobel prize.

Mutatis mutandis – The necessary changes being made. 'You must change your underwear.' (Italian, 'le mutande' = underwear.)

Ceteris paribus – Other things being equal. What goes on in Albania.

Hoi polloi – The many. You are one of the few, the **oligoi**, who knows the difference.

Otium cum dignitate – Ease with dignity. That which is not provided by the State Earnings Related Pension Scheme. The life of an MEP.

Gnothi seauton – Know thyself. What marathon runners say as they come to the 16,000th pain barrier.

Non omnis moriar – I shall not wholly die. Your response to the question 'Do you believe in God?'

Sub specie aeternitatis – Under the eye of eternity. What politicians forget.

Quot homines, tot sententiae – There are as many opinions as there are people to hold them. How you dismiss anyone who disagrees with you.

Vox populi, vox dei – The voice of the people is the voice of God. Patent nonsense.

Sequor non inferior – I follow, but am not inferior. The delusion of most middle management.

Petitio principii – Begging the question. The logical fallacy of assuming what has to be proved. Contemporary journalism.

Summa sedes non capit duos – The highest seat will not admit two. What President Clinton and his First Lady are finding out.

Mens sana in corpore sano – A healthy mind in a healthy body. A lobotomised jogger.

Semper cedentia retro – Always going forwards backwards. The modern world.

Venit summa dies et ineluctabile tempus – The last day and the ineluctable time are upon us. What Jehovah's Witnesses have been saying for years and years.

THE AUTHOR

Ross Leckie caught on to the Classics in AD 1962 at the precocious age of five. Ostracised to a school in the wilds of Kincardineshire, he soon realised that little competition in the Classics meant much opportunity.

At Oxford he found that the torch of Classical exegesis burned brightly but that most Classicists had bad breath and worked all the time.

To avoid such questions as 'Do you mean modern Greek?' he has variously farmed, taught, roughnecked, engaged in politics and written the award-winning historical novel *Hannibal*. Its sequel, *Scipio,* which sounds like the biography of a kangaroo but isn't, came next – as, he observes, sequels often do – and the third part of the trilogy, *Carthage*, is due out soon if it isn't already.

Now it's per ardua ad astra with novels on Aristotle and Dido. When he is not writing them, he works as director of communications for an Edinburgh investment management company and reviews for *The Times*. Or so he says.